Chosen to Worship
21 Days of Prayer

Dr. Amanda Goodson

ISBN-13: 978-0997875737

ISBN-10: 0997875739

Printed in the U.S.A.

Second Edition

ACKNOWLEDGEMENTS

Thank You, God, for allowing me to serve You in such a manner as is pleasing to You. I pray that I will find favor in Your sight as I share these stories with others and that they may also be blessed. I am grateful for my family, for their dedication to me, and all that God has allowed me to do.

Thank you, to Diane Snell, Connie Teague, Je're Harmon and Rosalyn Chapple for being significant contributors to this ministry effort. Trinity Temple CME Church, thank you!

TABLE OF CONTENTS

INTRODUCTION

Worship of God is special and significant in our daily lives. Those who worship God will have a heartfelt closeness to God through Jesus Christ. The Holy Spirit will continue to embrace those who worship God completely. John's gospel Chapter 4 verses 23-24, shares with us this important and vital actuality about worship… [23] *Yet a time is coming and has now come when the true worshipers will worship the Father in the Spirit and in truth, for they are the kind of worshipers the Father seeks.* [24] *God is spirit, and his worshipers must worship in the Spirit and in truth.*"

God's heart rests with those who worship. God is a jealous God and He wants your adoration and admiration of Him to be your total source. He wants us to seek after Him with our total hearts. When we seek God with our all, we have the ability to get into His presence, reverence and honor Him, and then go deeper in our relationship with Him. From the moment we desire God and want to worship Him, He will meet us and carry us to new dimensions of love, peace and joy. Worship will:

- Unlock your kingdom potential
- Catapult you into another place
- Turn you into a better person
- Destroy yokes of bondage
- Build you up spiritually
- Embrace you with a hedge of God's love

The *21 Days of Worship* comprises a daily journey of revelation through prayer into that place where we can become one with God and reach a place where we find divine comfort, access, healing and results. Every believer desires to be able to pray better and become comfortable doing so. This daily walk will gently guide the reader in taking a practical and applicable journey of relationship-building in order to reach that goal. The intent of this book is that the reader be able to accomplish this by utilizing relevant stories that demonstrate how we live and how we are made better because of a true relationship with Jesus Christ our Savior.

When you have true worship, there is intimacy with God, Himself. This relationship will birth:

- Blessing
- Anointing
- Shalom (Peace)
- Prophecy
- Deliverance and healing
- Miracles, signs and wonders
- Kingdom authority

I invite you to take this daily journey and to see how your life can and will be transformed through worship, prayer and thanksgiving. It is guaranteed that, through a daily commitment to prayer, your life will be changed, your relationship with God will be enhanced, and you will see the difference that this will make in your worship. Please read one chapter each day and document your reflections accordingly. At the end of the 21 days, share with your kingdom sisters and brothers how God has done marvelous things through this time with Him.

Day 1

What is Worship?

Purpose:

To understand that we are to ascribe worth and to give glory and thanks to our Most High God.

Hearing the Word:

Psalm 96

[1] Sing to the LORD a new song; sing to the LORD, all the earth.
[2] Sing to the LORD, praise his name; proclaim his salvation day after day.
[3] Declare his glory among the nations, his marvelous deeds among all peoples.
[4] For great is the LORD and most worthy of praise; he is to be feared above all gods.
[5] For all the gods of the nations are idols, but the LORD made the heavens.
[6] Splendor and majesty are before him; strength and glory are in his sanctuary.

⁷ Ascribe to the LORD, all you families of nations, ascribe to the LORD glory and strength.

⁸ Ascribe to the LORD the glory due his name; bring an offering and come into his courts.

⁹ Worship the LORD in the splendor of his [a] holiness; tremble before him, all the earth.

¹⁰ Say among the nations, "The LORD reigns." The world is firmly established, it cannot be moved; he will judge the peoples with equity.

¹¹ Let the heavens rejoice, let the earth be glad; let the sea resound, and all that is in it.

¹² Let the fields be jubilant, and everything in them; let all the trees of the forest sing for joy.

¹³ Let all creation rejoice before the LORD, for he comes, he comes to judge the earth. He will judge the world in righteousness and the peoples in his faithfulness.

Worship in Spirit and in Truth:

The English word "worship" is derived from Old English *worthscipe*, meaning 'worthiness' or 'worth-ship'. In its simplest concept, worship is to give worth to something. Christian worship is not simply giving worth to 'some thing', but it is focused on the Almighty, Triune God, because of who God is and all that He has done. As is revealed in the many names of God, used throughout the scriptures, worship that is ascribing worth to God, involves a multiplicity of actions on our part.

Some of those actions can be revealed in a few Hebrew terms that demonstrate both the many dimensions of the concept of worship and the range of responses or actions in expressing our worship to God.

Halal. The most commonly used word in the Old Testament, means to make a loud, clear sound of praise; to celebrate. The word _"hallelujah"_ comes from a combination of the Hebrew words Halal and Yahweh (or Yah).

Yadah and Todah. Both come from the root word _yad_, meaning "hand", and they are expressions of worship involving the use of our hands: to hold out one's hands, or to give thanks or revere with extended hands in thanksgiving, praise and adoration. This can also be used to mean to use your hands in confession or absolute surrender to God.

Barak. Comes from the root word _berech_ which means "knee." This act of worship involves kneeling down before God. It can also mean to congratulate, salute, praise or thank, and it implies giving reverence to God as an act of adoration.

Shachah. Means to bow, stoop down or to prostrate oneself as an act of submission or reverence; to make obeisance or to fall or bow down in reverence before God.

Tehillah. This is related to the word _halal_, and it means to offer praise and celebration by using hymns or songs of praise. It can also mean to sing spontaneous new songs to God by adding words to a melody from your heart.

Zamar. Means touching the strings or parts of musical instruments, and it is used as an expression of worship in the playing of instruments accompanied by voices, to celebrate or give praise with instruments and voices.

11

Shabach. Means to address in a loud tone, implying laud, praise or proclamation with a loud voice or a shout.

These are some of the most common Hebrew terms that describe worship. However, there are no limitations with worship. Worship can be demonstrated using every means and expression that is available to us. Some of those means can come through all kinds of gifts, music, instruments, movement, art, color, light, sound and language; just to name a few.

Worship is not limited by or defined to location or distance. When Jesus was asked about where one should worship, His response was that true worshippers must worship the Father in spirit and in truth. What that means is that worship has less to do with location or context, than the content and the heart of worship.

The two most important primary elements of true worship are **spirit** and **truth**.

Story:

When Nicodemus heard that he must be "born again," there was confusion all around concerning this prospect. Although he had been separated many years from his first birth, the thought of being born again brought it to his remembrance. When we think of the greatness of God and the newness of life, it brings to mind new life and new beginnings. The thoughts and cries of new babies bring smiles, and the thoughts of new life bring joy. Though most of us don't remember our birth moments or that moment in history when we were born, we love stories of our young years.

This Psalm reminds us of all the "good" and "new" things we like. We also think about the children and how Jesus said that in order to enter the Kingdom of God, we must come to Him as children. Children are enthusiastic about life. Even small, innocent babies marvel at the meeting and greeting of a new born child. This healthy, chubby child will learn to grow and trust its parents who are stronger and steady in their belief system. God our Father is strong and mighty and capable of teaching us to endure all trials and tribulations, but we must be willing to take small, baby steps toward maturing into sound biblically based worshiping adults. Worship is giving to the Lord all the adoration and obedience (bowed down) for being our Maker, Creator and Lord.

As we grow, our worship and identity with God also grows. The helpless little infant becomes the strong, mighty tree that is capable of sustaining life and developing a lifetime relationship with God. The mature worshiper approaches his/her relationship with God in a more resolute manner. Babies must be taught to read and write for years before being allowed to stand alone. Mature children of God come to know God and are rooted in their faith. They become unshakeable in their faith and relationship with God. To contrast, a 16-year old young adult approaches God from a different perspective than that of a 6-year old child. The 25-year old adult approaches God from a different perspective than that of a 16-year old.

Over the years I have watched my son become a strong man in God. He is no longer blown every which way trying to understand how to have a wonderful relationship with God and how to show his love and need for God. He is rooted and sound in the Lord and able to recognize what are the things of God that surround him. He recognizes the created things of God, the goodness that is in them, and he praises God for these things. He knows that God is strong when we are weak, and that God's power and love will sustain us in our weakness. He can discern the splendor of God around him in his daily walk with God.

We are all told to acknowledge the things of God. The New and Old Testaments testify to the splendor of God. Isaiah Chapter 6 says, *"His robe filled the temple."* We are all to magnify the Lord as we journey into total worship and submission to the wonderful love of our Creator.

Are you ready for the greatest journey of your life; walking in the presence of Almighty God; covered by the blood of His Son Jesus Christ, as you allow God to shape and prune you for His purpose and goal?

The entire universe speaks to the ability of God to do this marvelous thing in your life. Your love and worship will be taken to a higher level like never before seen in your life.

Worship God in the splendor of His glory! Worship God in the newness of life. Worship God as a renewed individual, trusting and believing in His strength and might! Bow down and submit before Almighty God.

Find that place in the universe that allows you to connect spiritually to the love of God, and then worship God with love and thanksgiving!

Ready to write?

Today's Date:

_____

_____

_____

_____

_____

_____

_____

_____

_____

_____

_____

_____

_____

_____

_____

_____

_____

_____

_____

Day 2

Why is Worship Important?
(I go beyond the seen realm into a deeper experience with God)

Purpose:

To understand that God demands (requires) it, He deserves it, and that He desires it.

Hearing the Word:

Exodus 34:14

[14] Do not worship any other god, for the LORD, whose name is Jealous, is a jealous God.

Story:

It is our responsibility to create the right atmosphere in relationship with God. Worship creates a place for God to inhabit and bless us. Scripture speaks of the "secret" place in which you can commune with God. A place of your choosing, physical or spiritual where you go to be alone with the Lord. In recent times we are to become familiar again with arranging a place of private worship with God. Remember, it does not have to be elaborate; just a place where you find that the peace of God inhabits. I have often told the story of praying in the bathroom when I need a quick place of quiet and refuge. I know that most people find a closet or even the sanctuary of their church to be the place where they can sit in God's presence to worship him. The place is important, but not as important as the worship itself. The bible passages about worshiping wooden idols and other "small" insignificant gods is somewhat sad. It is also an eye opener as to the care needed when choosing to worship the one and only God of creation.

We note that this age, and the ages before the technology, allows for marvelous invented things to be misused and wrongly identified as items to be worshipped. Make no mistake about it, if you know our Lord and Savior Jesus Christ, then you know that worship belongs to God. The Old and New Testaments verify the greatness of the one and only God. As stated in the scripture, He is a jealous God; and rightfully so.

Remember, when you first started dating and found that special person to love. You also wanted that person all to yourself. My girl friends always talk about how they "selected" the right guy to marry. I talk about my "list" of attributes that my husband had to meet in order to be considered for that awesome position in my life. The standard was set high, the expectation was that the "man of my dreams" would be awesome in every way. When I met him and married him, I knew that God had chosen him for me because my list became lost in the love that I had for him. Oh, yes, I did tell him all about my list, but in my love for him I forgot to keep track of which items he met or exceeded. Love keeps no list of wrongs. God has a higher and more stringent list of qualifications that we can meet or exceed. He is a jealous God and will not share us with false idols. There are no exceptions to this rule. If God kept a list, we would not be able to meet nor exceed the requirements. Only His Son Jesus holds the standard of perfect. We, however, are loved by God for who we are, and as we grow and mature in Him, we learn to worship Him in the beauty of His holiness as the only true desire of our hearts.

Marriage is worshiping God. God's presence is in every aspect of a marriage. I have been married to the love of my life for 20 years now. The years seem less because we have spent them together. We both have a love relationship with God and have passed that passion on to our son. Our human nature is to look for the right mate with whom we can marry, and in the eyes of God, become one. This union is a celebration in which God can participate and we can flourish.

My friend, Lisa, had been married to the "guy next door" for over 35 years. She told me the stories of their early years of dating and marriage. It is fantastic to laugh with friends over what we call the "silliness" of the early dating years when we were "jealous" of our mates. At some point, we decided that they should only belong to us and to no one else. We should be the center of their lives, and no one else. As a Pastor, I have the opportunity to serve God in the marriage ceremony. It is a wondrous feeling to stand front and center and have couples declare their love for one another before God and the world. When two lovers are joined, the effect extends outside the relationship they have with each other. The joy, the laughter, the smiles, the sharing, and reshaping that happens when two people join families making them stronger and holy in the eyes of God is tremendous. God's love is present. The love that emanates through their union is of God and ordained by Him. I understand how God would be jealous if this love is worldly and lies outside of His decree and plan.

This is what God is saying to us about being focused on our relationship with Him, and no one else, when we worship. We should focus on a living, giving, and loving God; not some inanimate object which is not able to create or sustain life. Remember, the bible story of the wood that was chopped down, carved into an idol then used as kindling for a fire? It also perished. Our God is not like this in any form of the imagination. God is the same God, yesterday, today and tomorrow. Our worship of this great, loving God is not in vain. To love and be loved is outstanding and fulfilling. How we share this love is accomplished through worshipping the God Who commanded and designed us to love.

It is a wonderful moment when a family starts to expand, and God is seen in the eyes of a child. Children learn to share the God of their parents, with siblings, family and friends. Worship brings family and loved ones closer together in God. From watching others, children learn to worship in a specific obedient manner. They learn about the love of God and the character of God and are able to see this all manifest in their parents. Children learn to share God at an early age and the joy of serving an enormous God. God loves unconditionally and as long as He is the focus of our love, meaning that our love is

20

centered on Him, He is a giving and wonderful God. The scripture says that God is a jealous God. However, the beauty of this statement is that through our obedience and worship, God is love and is a loving God.

Ready to write?

Today's Date:

_____

_____

_____

_____

_____

_____

_____

_____

_____

_____

_____

_____

_____

_____

Day 3

What Does Worship Look Like for Me as an Individual?
(I prepare a place for God to manifest Himself)

Purpose:

To establish and identify a purpose, priority, and a place where worship is to begin.

Hearing the Word:

Psalm 95:6

[6] Come, let us bow down in worship; Let us kneel before the LORD our Maker.

Story:

The sanctuary of our church is a beautiful place to worship God. It is shrouded with tradition and love for God. It contains all the new technology that allows us to reach this generation on their own terms. The decrees and demands for this generation is drastically different from the others,

23

as it should be, and has been with previous generations. As seen throughout history, everything has changed, not only within the secular world, but also in how and when we worship. Read the following statements in the context of understanding the outcomes of your worship:

- No worship – no power.
- Little worship – little power.
- Exceptional worship – exceptional power.
- Eliminate all distractions, inconveniences and focus on God alone.
- Uplift the name of Jesus as my spiritual act of worship.
- Pursue God with all my might....

This is the mantra of a whole new generation who moves at the speed of time. Everything moves faster and in a shorter time frame. Faster is better and even faster than fast is much better for the generation of ever changing technology. Keeping pace with the changes is an everyday challenge. The question of how our worship keeps up with these changes had been the subject of many a sermon. We are told to embrace the change and can see how technology has infiltrated the church setting. For some bibles are electronic books, which are easy to access and the information within them is easily accessed. The big problem that arises for this techno-savvy generation is time management. News flash for many: the God that created all things (and all things that were created were created by God) God created time also and gives many options for managing it.

We call it corporate worship and for most it happens on one of the weekend days. Within most church denominations worship happens on a Saturday or Sunday: so do most of the important events of our lives. This time has also been deemed family time, or sports events time, or for a whole generation of people, it is known as "me" time. What we have discovered is that all this time is God's time. Worship is central to God's time. There is an old antidote that states, "The family that prays together-stays together it is applicable to several of our circumstances. We desire to grow our family and friends in the love of God through prayers and worship, and for this, time has to be allotted.

This all really sounds challenging, right? It really is not, it only requires setting our priorities. I say God should always be a priority. Navigating the world today has its own challenges; God at the center of our families keeps everyone on track to His peace, eternal life and love.

How does worship impact our daily lives? The challenge of keeping up in this techno-marvelous world is the stresses of everyday living, but only for those who do not set standards and priorities. Again, with God at the center, there are His blessings and favor to be added. The fantastic thing is that we determine how much God to add. For me and my family God is the main ingredient in life: no worship-no power, is not an option as we traverse the jungle of everyday life. It is often God's love and power that gets us through the pits and pitfalls of our lives. We rejoice and receive His blessings with thanksgiving and supplication, prayer and fasting.

I encourage people to begin (and end) their day with worship to God who sets the sun and the moon in the heavenlies. Pray that God orders your steps according to His Word so that you don't stumble. Focus on the events of your day with the strength of focused Godly worship. In worship, you are able to have conversation with God who predestined you to go through the day.

Here is a truth and dare question for you. How much time do you spend in worship to your Creator, God? Personally, I too don't have enough time in a day to worship God as I desire. My 24-hour day would be 24 hours of worship. However, prioritizing allows me to place God in first and last position. I worship Him first in the morning (ok and throughout my day) and lastly before going to bed. Worshiping changes your life and your attitude, which we often say, also changes your altitude. Worship starts your day on a positive note with permission from God to proceed in this joy throughout the day. If you should encounter a negative counter force return to you last stage of worship before proceeding through your day. Worship that ends your day is thankfulness for both the day behind you and the one ahead. Never trudge through the days of your life alone, take God with you.

Up lift Jesus as the original cross bearer. He showed us how to accomplish this task. First with endurance and then with steadfast focus on our Father God. Never forget the cross that Jesus bore for us; it will help you when you feel persecuted to know that he made it through that period for us. God has promised never to leave nor forsake us.

Maria tells Mike's story as one of those head-scratching, bewildering stories when reminiscing about Mike's impact on her life. Mike was a person of great world wealth. Back in the day, Mike would have been known as the man with

26

the green (money producing) thumbs. He had more money than he would every use in his life time, in fact, rumor had it that Mike was so rich he would not have to work for 2 or 3 lifetimes. One day Mike showed up wanting to fine Jerrod. He was determined to get the $3,641.45 that Jerrod owed to him. He was angry that it had not been returned as promised. He ranted on and on about how he had trusted the guy and not being repaid. Mike seemed frustrated, angry to the point that he was yelling when the told Maria the story. He wanted her help in locating Jerrod.

She had not seen him this angry over money before. In fact, in earlier days, they had talked about money and the root to which it was attached and how it would never be a controlling factor in their lives. Today Mike was angry about this deal he had made with Jerrod, and she wanted to know why. So, in the tradition of true friendship, she asked him why he was so determined to find Jerrod and "rip him a new one." Mike blurted out at her that he had been diagnosed with an illness and was given a bad report. "I don't have long to live," he shouted from the top of his lungs. It took her a minute to respond as only a friend would. "And you are wanting this money for what?" she asked. "You can't take it with you. Surely Jerrod will write you a check, especially if he knows that you can't cash it! Mike's focus was on the wrong thing.

At that moment, God would have been a better person for him to focus his time and resources on. Mike spent months battling his illness, but he was never alone. Together with God, they fought the good fight and won. Did he get his money from Jerrod? I don't think it crossed his mind much over the next few years! He chose to battle for his life in worship!

How much time do you spend in worship? Review the chart below, and add to your worship time as you can.

Ready to write?

LINE-UP™ Inventory			
Little Worship -Little Power	No Worship -No Power	Exceptional Worship - Exceptional Power	Uplift Jesus
How will you worship God more in your life?	What will you do to worship daily?	Exceptional worshippers see tremendous moves of God. What will you do to pursuer exceptional worship?	List ways you can uplift the name of Jesus today!

Today's Date:

_____

_____

_____

_____

_____

_____

_____

_____

Day 4

What Does Worship Look Like for My Church Family?

Purpose:

To know the importance of individual, as well as, corporate and familial worship.

Hearing the Word:

Psalm 86:8-12

[8] Among the gods there is none like you, Lord; no deeds can compare with yours.
[9] All the nations you have made will come and worship before you, Lord; they will bring glory to your name.
[10] For you are great and do marvelous deeds; you alone are God.
[11] Teach me your way, LORD, that I may rely on your faithfulness; give me an undivided heart, that I may fear your name.
[12] I will praise you, Lord my God, with all my heart; I will glorify your name forever.

Story:

Meeting Lisa was an experience in itself. She is a unique person dedicated to God in every aspect of her life. She always shares the fact that she comes from a worshiping family. Several brothers, sisters, cousins, aunts and uncles are pastors and ministers in the church. Lisa has, what I will call, a God-knowing family. To have that many people in one family involved in ministry is unique.

Cheryl says that ministers are sprinkled throughout her family. She grew up knowing who God is and who He purposed her to be.

Cassandra, on the other hand, is the only minister in her family. Her family worships together, but no one else has heeded the calling to ministry.

For many of us, the church family is our family of worship. The time we spend in bible study and Sunday morning worship service is our family's corporate worship time. Praise and worship is not limited to Sunday mornings or Wednesday night bible study. Praying for and with other church members should be a priority for the church family. Remember, the antidote from earlier chapters: the family that prays together stays together. Worshipping with the church should be the normal thing to do. Often times we know our church family better that our biological family. Good, bad or indifferent, who better to worship with you than the people you stand with in the church? These people know the church vision, church mission, church history, and most importantly they know you.

Pastors present the vision and mission of a church to the entire church body. Members become aligned with it and subdue it together. Members become accountability partners and co-worshipers for the things and knowledge of God. Under the guidance of a shepherd, the flock learns together and becomes family for many people within the church. Church organizations support the church members, and they are usually loving toward one another.

Worshipping together is the family coming together in one accord to magnify God and show our affection towards our Father, King, Lord, Provider and Priest. He has done marvelous things for us!

Ready to write?

Today's Date:

_____

_____

_____

_____

_____

_____

_____

_____

_____

_____

_____

Day 5

What Does Worship Look Like In My Church?

Purpose:

To understand the importance of worship demonstrated freely in the dance.

Hearing the Word:

2 Samuel 6:14-15

[14] Wearing a linen ephod, David was dancing before the LORD with all his might,
[15] while he and all Israel were bringing up the ark of the LORD with shouts and the sound of trumpets.

Story:

The music lyrics tout, "When the spirit of the Lord comes upon my heart, I will dance like David danced." Having someone dance before the Lord in today's church setting seems the norm. I can imagine the surprise of David's subjects when he danced with great joy before the Lord. There are scholars among you who would say David had great reasons to dance as he did, because the Lord had brought him to great heights. David went from the fields to the palace; all at the direction of God. He was a man of great wealth and possessions, and he served God as King of Israel.

Those appear to be great reasons to dance. I would also like to remind you that David also lamented greatly before God. The Psalms that David wrote seem to portray him as a sad man. His joy and his sorrow are very evident in the Psalms; enough to make one want to dance before the God who saved him through his many trials and tribulations. David also dances as honor to God. He was allowed to return God's resting place back to Jerusalem. That was an honorable thing to have accomplished in his lifetime, but we know David accomplished much to the glory of God.

Our testimonies are powerful tools for opening up the eyes of others to the love of God. Jesus (David's descendant) saved, healed, and changed many lives; beginning with His disciples. We have been redeemed of sin through the redemptive work of Jesus; David's descendant.

Read David's story and discover that David had much to worship God for and he did. What limitations have you put on your worship? David worshipped for more than just his generation. He knew that his son would be in a position to honor God in a way far greater than he had. Although we say that worship should be vertical, be aware that you are being watched by the next generation. Teach them verbally, mentally and physically to worship God with all their might, without limitation or hindrance.

David danced generations ago, but his dancing still has an impact today. There was a time when there were no praise dancers in the church. Look at us now. Over time, it has become the norm. It is not the dancer, but the worshipping of God that is at hand. A whole generation of dancers received a birthing in the Spirit.

Join me in encouraging others to dance as David danced. Today there are professional dance techniques and styles; however, the end result (honoring God) has been maintained and it has become an intuitive way to honor God. Worship God in your way; ensure that you are worshiping Him in spirit and in truth.

In the year of my 5th anniversary, I remember a dancer from Chicago who traveled to Tucson to honor her mother and present to me a praise dance as a gift. The gift was awesomely presented to the entire congregation. On that day, we had several local dancers who also danced in honor of the event and before the Lord. God is not a God of limitations. Dance is another form of worship, and it employs several different techniques. We have often used flags at our church and allowed the children to dance.

Ready to write?

DANCe™ Inventory			
Determine your worship toward God alone	**Always seek His face**	**Never stop worshipping**	**Center your thoughts on adoring God!**
How can you determine to worship God alone?	In what ways may God ask you to seek him today?	Is there anything more important than God?	List three ways you may think more about God today!

Today's Date:

_____

_____

_____

_____

_____

_____

_____

_____

_____

Day 6

God the Father, Son and Holy Spirit is Worthy of our Worship

Purpose:

To recognize that worship is about the power of love within yourself.

Hearing the Word:

1 Corinthians 13:4-8, 13

Love is patient, love is kind. It does not envy, it does not boast, it is not proud. It does not dishonor others, it is not self-seeking, it is not easily angered, it keeps no record of wrongs. Love does not delight in evil but rejoices with the truth. It always protects, always trusts, always hopes, always perseveres. ...And now these three remain: faith, hope and love. But the greatest of these is love.

Story:

Paul in 1 Corinthians defines perfect love. It is an awesome thing that his description truly defines our first love. Our first love is that which was given as a result of the events that occurred in the Garden of Eden. The Genesis creation story does not mention the love that God had when He was creating the world. It does not mention the love that God had when forming Adam, or when creating Eve for Adam. God looked upon the creation that He had formed from the dust of the earth and the bone of man, and then said it was very good. He greatly and graciously expresses His love for His creation in the narrative of the transition of fallen man to redeemed man. The first love that God has for His creation is shown in the statement that answers the question of why He (God) redeemed man.

"For God so loved the world that he gave His only begotten Son that whosoever believes shall have eternal life." The love of God for mankind is the first love. It is by imitation that we first receive true, unconditional love. It comes first from our parents. This love and the willingness to obey God is seen in Abraham, a man God called righteous. As an obedient servant, Abraham was willing to make the pilgrimage up to an area where he was to sacrifice his son to God. But as we are often told, God had a "ram in the bush" blessing for Abraham's obedience. Love is a two-way bond between God the Creator and man His creation. However, God requires more. When asked, what is the greatest command, Jesus answered, *"That you love your God."*

What is unconditional love? When we read the scripture, we should look at our relationships and question whether they meet the standard set forth. Are we truly loving, as defined in 1 Corinthians 13:4-8, 13? A more profound study would be, can we truly love everyone this way? We love our husbands, wives, children and friends as described in this scripture. I would hope that we all aspire toward this type of love.

Ready to write?

POWR™ of Love Inventory		
Personally Owned by God	**Willing**	**Ready**
What does God's Personal Ownership of you mean to you?	In what ways are you Willing to love? List three.	Are you Ready to love God, others and yourself, knowing that love will never fail?

Today's Date:

_____

_____

_____

_____

_____

_____

_____

_____

Day 7

Worship God Through Tough Times

Purpose:

To gain assurance that true worship guarantees protection and provision.

Hearing the Word:

Psalm 34

[1] I will extol the Lord at all times; his praise will always be on my lips.
[2] I will glory in the Lord; let the afflicted hear and rejoice.
[3] Glorify the Lord with me; let us exalt his name together.
[4] I sought the Lord, and he answered me; he delivered me from all my fears.
[5] Those who look to him are radiant; their faces are never covered with shame.
[6] This poor man called, and the Lord heard him; he saved him out of all his troubles.
[7] The angel of the Lord encamps around those who fear him, and he delivers them.
[8] Taste and see that the Lord is good; blessed is the one who takes refuge in him.

⁹ Fear the Lord, you his holy people, for those who fear him lack nothing.

¹⁰ The lions may grow weak and hungry, but those who seek the Lord lack no good thing.

¹¹ Come, my children, listen to me; I will teach you the fear of the Lord.

¹² Whoever of you loves life and desires to see many good days,

¹³ keep your tongue from evil and your lips from telling lies.

¹⁴ Turn from evil and do good; seek peace and pursue it.

¹⁵ The eyes of the Lord are on the righteous, and his ears are attentive to their cry;

¹⁶ but the face of the Lord is against those who do evil, to blot out their name from the earth.

¹⁷ The righteous cry out, and the Lord hears them; he delivers them from all their troubles.

¹⁸ The Lord is close to the brokenhearted and saves those who are crushed in spirit.

¹⁹ The righteous person may have many troubles, but the Lord delivers him from them all;

²⁰ he protects all his bones, not one of them will be broken.

²¹ Evil will slay the wicked; the foes of the righteous will be condemned.

²² The Lord will rescue his servants; no one who takes refuge in him will be condemned.

Story:

Exalt the Lord with me! Blessed is the one who takes refuge in Him. I love reading passages in my bible that offer an immediate blessing. Read line 8 of this Psalm. First, it says taking refuge is sweet, and secondly it is a blessing! God says, I am God, there is no other like Me.

42

So, while you are going through your stuff, I will give you another reason to feel secure and know that I am not far away from you. Isn't it a wonderful thought to know that God is not far away during troubled times. In fact, you are invited to take refuge in Him during those harsh troubled times. Having troubles does not make you unworthy of God's blessing; just the opposite is true. So, take care to heed the stipulations of this psalm. Our troubles often bring us closer to God.

A friend and I were talking when he said, "What is the first thing you do when troubles rear their ugly head?"

> [1] I will extol the LORD at all times;
> His praise will always be on my lips.

All good things come from God. Praising God during the good times is an easy thing to do. Rejoice, rejoice, and rejoice in the good days. What happens during the not so good times? The psalmist says there should be no difference. We should glorify God continuously; no matter the state of our personal lives. Come, he says; let us exalt His name together. Then, he says, let me give you an example of what the Lord can do during times of trial when you seek Him out. He will deliver you from your fears, and He will save you out of your troubles.

Is the fear of the Lord the beginning of wisdom? How lovely when we have reverential fear of God. He sends His angels to watch over us, to encamp around us and deliver us. Does God send an angel to deliver us from our trails? If you don't believe it, put it to the test. Go to God with your troubles, and see if He delivers you from them.

Delivery from troubled times is a blessing. Listen and learn, he says; the instructions on how to gain this release is also included in the psalm. Here is the breakdown:

- Fear the Lord and lack nothing
- Seek the Lord and lack nothing

We are taught to seek God with all of our heart. There is no better way to know God than through His Word and His promises, developing a strong prayer life along the way. The scripture says seek the Lord while He may be found. Often this is noted as an indication that there will come a time when He may not easily be found. The scriptures also say that when you seek God, He will also seek you; noting that God is also interested in building a relationship with you. Seek the Lord and lack nothing means God will supply your every need. What an awesome relationship you would have; one built on trust and care, and both parties being themselves and looking out for one another!

Listen and be taught to fear the Lord. Listen to the Word of God and have a reverential fear of Him. We are commanded to love; but not selfishly, and to love unconditionally with self-control and without malice. Obedience, kindness, gentleness are characteristic of those we choose to love. It requires that we take a self-inventory and ask the question: Am I the person I want everyone else to be? Love not your life; love God. Bridle your tongue and speak no evil against others. Learn to love through God. Turn from evil and seek to do good. Acknowledge that God created us all and that you are not perfect, but striving to be better. Go to God with the troubles of your days, and God will hear your heart. Do no evil, for evil is not of God and not in the plan that He has for your life. Allow healing for those past hurts. Remember, God heals, protects, and delivers the righteous person. Take refuge under His wing in times of trouble. The enemy shall flee from you when you call upon the Name of God. God says I know the plans I have for you. His plans are greater than yours. God created us to worship Him not self. Walk through life with God.

Ready to write?

Tuff™ Inventory			
Trust God for everything	**Understand that He knows all**	**Forgive**	**Forget**
How can you trust God more today?	List 3 challenges you are facing and present them totally before God.	Is there anyone you need to forgive? Do it now.	Forget those things behind and press for a high call. Do you agree?

Today's Date:

_____

_____

_____

_____

_____

_____

_____

Day 8

The Call to Worship

Purpose:

To know that entrance into God's presence comes after love and trust.

Hearing the Word:

2 Kings 17:36-39

[36] But the LORD, who brought you up out of Egypt with mighty power and outstretched arm, is the one you must worship. To him you shall bow down and to him offer sacrifices.
[37] You must always be careful to keep the decrees and regulations, the laws and commands he wrote for you. Do not worship other gods.
[38] Do not forget the covenant I have made with you, and do not worship other gods.
[39] Rather, worship the LORD your God; it is he who will deliver you from the hand of all your enemies."

Story:

Worship and bowing down before God is an act of submission. Positional prayer builds a personal relationship with God. There is no required position for prayer. God hears our prayers and is honored and reacts to them when they are humbly submitted. One of the first things we do is to teach our children to pray. Often we go as far as teaching them the prayer position. The position, praying down on your knees, holds as a sacred position. Children are taught this is a sacred position, and it allows them to call upon the Lord.

As children, we were given a rhythmic version of a prayer that was used for night prayer.
Now I lay me
Down to sleep
I pray, dear Lord
My soul to keep.

At this point in our lives, worship becomes more personal. We worship in accordance with our understanding, and present ourselves to God in humbled adoration. As we matured in God and our knowledge and needs changed, then our worship and prayer also matured, was changed and became more personal. Prayer time increased and became more specific and confidential. The kneeling position is shared with the position of walking around a room. We bring before God the desires of our heart. We pour out our love for God and for others before Him; sometimes in celebration or in supplication and thanksgiving.

48

It is our love and trust of God that allows us to enter into the sacred place of open and honest worship to Him and complete adoration for His power and ability to respond to us on a personal basis. The love of God can be heard in one's prayer. The free flow of prayer entices others to join in and begin to serve God in spirit and in truth.

The covenant promise of not worshipping other gods was broken by Israel several times in biblical history. This was not pleasing to God, and is avoided by prayer warriors today.

Public displays of worship are still being done during altar calls. Corporately, people gather at the altar and pray to God. God, in His infinite wisdom, holds fast to the covenant He has made with Israel, and He listens to His people.

We pray for others and ourselves; specifically, our brothers and sisters in Christ. There are no limitations to our prayers, as we tend to lay all that impacts our lives before Almighty God. As prayer warriors and intercessors, we are called to continuous prayer before God. Scripture says, *"Let everything that has breath, praise the Lord."*

Prayer warriors like Evan spend hours praying for God to bless others. Evan is a quiet soul, but he believes it is not necessary to yell. He trusts God and reports to have seen many miracles during his life and walk with God.

Ready to write?

Cal'd™ Inventory		
In what ways do you see yourself chosen to worship God?	Attitude	Love your self and others
How can you trust God more today?	List ways your attitude should change today that may hinder your worship?	How may you act more loving today? List 1-3 ways below.

Today's Date:

_____

_____

_____

_____

_____

_____

_____

_____

_____

Day 9

My Response to Worship

Purpose:

To know that after love and trust, we can freely give our all with total assurance that God can and will do everything He promised to do.

Hearing the Word:

Genesis 22:1-18

[1] Some time later God tested Abraham. He said to him, "Abraham!" "Here I am," he replied.
[2] Then God said, "Take your son, your only son, whom you love—Isaac—and go to the region of Moriah. Sacrifice him there as a burnt offering on a mountain I will show you."
[3] Early the next morning Abraham got up and loaded his donkey. He took with him two of his servants and his son Isaac. When he had cut enough wood for the burnt offering, he set out for the place God had told him about. [4] On the third day Abraham looked up and saw the place in the distance.

⁵ He said to his servants, "Stay here with the donkey while I and the boy go over there. We will worship and then we will come back to you."

⁶ Abraham took the wood for the burnt offering and placed it on his son Isaac, and he himself carried the fire and the knife. As the two of them went on together,

⁷ Isaac spoke up and said to his father Abraham, "Father?" "Yes, my son?" Abraham replied. "The fire and wood are here," Isaac said, "but where is the lamb for the burnt offering?"

⁸ Abraham answered, "God himself will provide the lamb for the burnt offering, my son." And the two of them went on together.

⁹ When they reached the place God had told him about, Abraham built an altar there and arranged the wood on it. He bound his son Isaac and laid him on the altar, on top of the wood.

¹⁰ Then he reached out his hand and took the knife to slay his son.

¹¹ But the angel of the LORD called out to him from heaven, "Abraham! Abraham!" "Here I am," he replied.

¹² "Do not lay a hand on the boy," he said. "Do not do anything to him. Now I know that you fear God, because you have not withheld from me your son, your only son."

¹³ Abraham looked up and there in a thicket he saw a ram caught by its horns. He went over and took the ram and sacrificed it as a burnt offering instead of his son.

¹⁴ So Abraham called that place The LORD Will Provide. And to this day it is said, "On the mountain of the LORD it will be provided."

¹⁵ The angel of the LORD called to Abraham from heaven a second time

¹⁶ and said, "I swear by myself, declares the LORD, that because you have done this and have not withheld your son, your only son,

¹⁷ I will surely bless you and make your descendants as numerous as the stars in the sky and as the sand on the

seashore. Your descendants will take possession of the cities of their enemies,

[18] and through your offspring all nations on earth will be blessed, because you have obeyed me."

Story:

When we read Abraham's story we see his character come to life. Abraham took his position of authority over all that God had graciously given him. He handled Lot with discernment and loved Sarah. In this part of the narrative, we see Abraham submit to God's request without question. This is admirable considering what God requested of Abraham. As parents, we cringe at the thought of such a request. As children of God, we question whether we would have the resolve of Abraham to carry out such a request. At the very core of Abraham's ability to conduct himself in such an honorable way is his relationship with God. At this juncture, Abraham had many encounters with God and has come to know that God will do what He says He will do. I venture to say, Abraham knew the love that God had for him, and more importantly, the love and trust that he, Abraham, had for God.

God kept His promises to Abraham, and everything that Abraham had belonged to God. He talked to God, and he had been blessed as God had promised. The birth of his son Isaac was only one promise among many that God had kept. God had required that Abraham move to a new land, and had blessed both Abraham and Lot in that new land. God had blessed Abraham in battle and allowed him the riches to tithe to the high priest. God had acknowledged and blessed his relationship with Sarah and kept the promise of a son and an heir to whom he could pass down all his riches and possessions of land and cattle. God had honored His Word and had given Sarah the desire of her heart by making her a birth mother. The son that she so longed for was now a living vibrant being whom they enjoyed daily.

Now we get to look at and learn from Abraham what obedience to Almighty God, the Creator of all things, would require and look like. Understanding and learning from this narrative may require reading it several times. Submission to the request of God began in a place called Haran. Abraham did as God directed and left his land. In this part of the story we learn of true obedience. Abraham teaches us obedience to God that came without question or rebuttal, and obedience to God given with humility and love.

Although several other questions arise from this narrative, this lesson's focus is Abraham's outstanding obedience, his sacrifice of a desired son, the sacrifice of his temperament and his heart, and of his loyalty to God. Note here that God did not require the sacrifice from both Abraham and Sarah. He only required that Abraham take Isaac up for the sacrifice.

Here we also review our relationship with God. The "what if" scenario begins. We also look deeper into our lives and answer a greater question of our own abilities to carry out this request. The similarity of what God would give to us all in sacrificing His only begotten Son stands out with boldness in this narrative. The thought that God would require Isaac to be a sacrifice, made by Abraham, immediately brings to mind the acts of Jesus and His sacrifice on the cross. Jesus, God's own Son, would

54

withstand the demeaning of the world to ransom all mankind from sin.

God began to reign in Abraham's life early in the first stages of their relationship. We know that this has become a relationship built of several outstanding principles. What type of relationship have you built with God? Is your relationship based on love and trust? These are two very powerful building blocks. Are you aware of the promises God has made and kept in your life? What promises have you made to God? Did you keep them?

As God guides Abraham through the scenario, we see certain outlying end results. We hear Abraham's conversations and know that he intends to bring Isaac home. God also uses Abraham and Isaac to teach us another lesson – obedience without questioning is a mighty key to our worship and relationship with God. Abraham's humbled, righteous, and loving characteristic of faithfulness stands out in this part of the narrative. This speaks of Abraham's unfailing love for God.

Is obedience greater than sacrifice? Abraham believes in God saving his son – no matter what; because his son was the promised seed through Abraham.

Here are some other thoughts for you to take to heart and points to ponder in worship:

- Obedience is key in worship!
- The Lord, Himself is involved in active worship – He will surely bless you. His promises to Abraham is part of your covenant:

- When God calls for something, He will provide for it Himself. On the mountain of the Lord, God will provide for you THIS day!
- There may be those around you who are not purposed to go up with you.
- Go up and worship. You will come back a blessed person.
- God will bless you because of your obedience,
- You will take possession of the cities of your enemies.
- The nations on the earth will be blessed through you.

- When you focus on God, your experience with Him and sensitivity to Him will be heightened and enlightened.
- Simply by reading this today, you are moving into another realm of worship that will cause your spirit to be reinvigorated, energized and renewed.
- Worship is a privilege and will happen with or without you.
- Choose your connections wisely; distractions may hinder your worship. Your assignment from this day forward is to eliminate distractions and not become one yourself. Not everyone will go to the level of worship that God will take you.
- Worshipping God means you should be more like Christ as disciples.
- You will find yourself going into an elevated sphere of influence when you worship God daily in your heart and with your mouth.
- True worship builds God an atmosphere to inhabit, and it aligns us with Him and makes Him high above all!

We know the outcome of the request that God made to Abraham. We shout with joy that it ended this way. We question whether or not we would be able to carry out such a request. I would like to say that being submitted to God as Abraham was, going through the trails that Abraham endured, and loving God as Abraham did might impact your decision. Is such a goal one you can aspire to have? God had a plan for Abraham, Sarah, Lot, Isaac and the generations to come in the lineage of Abraham. There were blessings to be had and character to be developed.

How about you, based upon the Abrahamic narrative, what changes do you discern in your life?

Ready to write?

Fill out the blanks below and describe how your AACT ™ of worship is shifting.

AACCT of Worship™ Inventory		
Adoration & Affection	**Choice & Commitment**	**Truth & Spirit**
What will you do to deepen your love & reverence for God?	What decisions will you make to desire and follow Christ more as an act of worship?	True worshippers worship in spirit and truth. In what ways might you change your worship focus?

Today's Date:

_____

_____

_____

_____

_____

_____

_____

_____

_____

_____

_____

_____

_____

_____

_____

_____

_____

_____

_____

Day 10

Chosen to Worship

Purpose:

To reach the place of knowing why there is a need for expectation of provision and protection in the face of trials and troubles.

Hearing the Word:

Genesis 32:22-30

> 22 That night Jacob got up and took his two wives, his two female servants and his eleven sons and crossed the ford of the Jabbok.
> 23 After he had sent them across the stream, he sent over all his possessions.
> 24 So Jacob was left alone, and a man wrestled with him till daybreak.
> 25 When the man saw that he could not overpower him, he touched the socket of Jacob's hip so that his hip was wrenched as he wrestled with the man.
> 26 Then the man said, "Let me go, for it is daybreak." But Jacob replied, "I will not let you go unless you bless me."
> 27 The man asked him, "What is your name?" "Jacob," he answered.

[28] Then the man said, "Your name will no longer be Jacob, but Israel, because you have struggled with God and with humans and have overcome."
[29] Jacob said, "Please tell me your name." But he replied, "Why do you ask my name?" Then he blessed him there.
[30] So Jacob called the place Peniel, saying, "It is because I saw God face to face, and yet my life was spared."

Story:

There are the things that we wrestle with these days, and then we find ourselves out-muscled and weak. Yet we know that we shall succeed if we just hold on. The bible states, *"When I am weak, He (God) is strong."* When you feel out-manned by the world just hold on! Often the weighty things of our lives seem too heavy for us to overcome.

Jacob was dealing with the safety of his family, the future of his family, encountering Esau, and leaving Laban. Then he was put into a position where his only resolve was to hold on to what he perceived was God. He did not defeat his foe; he merely held on until his subduer had to leave the encounter. There are times when the way out of a situation may not be clearly marked, and we can't find the exit sign. If God is in it, we simply need to hold on and allow Him to show us the way out.

In today's economy the testimonies are many. Hope is alive and intricately embedded in our everyday lives. Shana's story is similar to Jacobs, but her hope in God had been laid on the altar several times. She had lost her job that was vital, not only to her survival, but also to the many people she supported. Her savings was dwindling away because she chose to help others maintain during her down time. She knew that there was a job for her somewhere, anywhere; and that after a few months on the job, she would rebound. Her heart was saddened by the thought that she would someday have to tell her brother that she could no longer help with his medical needs, and the family who lived in her garage would have to vacate the house in two months if no job was forth coming. She had nowhere to turn; and most importantly to her, neither did they.

Prayer was her daily song. God had heard their plight for two years as her savings dwindled to nothing. Each month, every withdrawal was preceded with a prayer, followed with a prayer, and made reluctantly with a prayer. It was all they had so, she pressed forward. Her nights were filled with wrestling angels, but she knew God, and she had an awesome relationship with Him. When Satan came along to taunt her about the choices she had made, she retaliated immediately with the Words Jesus had spoken when He encountered Satan.

She had already questioned her choice and knew it was the right thing to do; therefore, she waited on God to show up. She knew without a doubt whom she served. Prayer, faith, and hope were her weapons of choice. As she saw her plans disappear, she knew God would provide for them all. The waiting was the test of her reliance.

When facing the trials and troubles we must hold on to God and to His promises. Jacob held on and placed a demand on his wrestling partner. As Shana waits to hear from God, she continues to do her best within the limits God has given her.

I will keep you posted on her plight. She, just like I, has an expectation that God will provide.

Ready to write?

Today's Date:

_____

_____

_____

_____

_____

_____

_____

_____

_____

_____

_____

_____

_____

_____

_____

_____

Day 11

Elevate Your Worship

Purpose:

To identify a path for progressing beyond what is 'ordinarily' expected for worship.

Hearing the Word:

Micah 4:6-8

> [6] "In that day," declares the LORD, "I will gather the lame; I will assemble the exiles and those I have brought to grief.
> [7] I will make the lame my remnant, those driven away a strong nation. The LORD will rule over them in Mount Zion from that day and forever.
> [8] As for you, watchtower of the flock, stronghold of Daughter Zion, the former dominion will be restored to you; kingship will come to Daughter Jerusalem."

Story:

One definition of the lame, as it relates to the church, is they are those who are not able to fully walk in the Word and ways of God. They shall be gathered along with those who are believers and have been barred from practicing their worship and praise to God, and they shall be assembled as a nation in which the Lord will be their only Ruler. Lord, God will rule forever! God will restore His people unto Himself!

Ally will argue that every wakening day is an opportunity to worship and praise God. "Sometimes we don't look like what the world thinks the children of God should look like," she quips! "See my mansion," she says. "Come let's worship the Lord together." Her worship is prayer, song, and dance before the Lord. Ally does it from her makeshift bed, refusing to go to a real shelter because she says there are poor people who need the beds. She is not one of them, even though she has no permanent roof over her head, very little money in her pocket, and often fills her stomach with a prayer. God is good. Where she is now in her walk on this earth is much better than where she was only a few years ago, according to her new standard. She lost her job and her house, but she never lost her belief in God nor her faith; although it takes a blow every now and then. Ally will retort with a wide smile and a warm heart: "Jesus suffered much more than I have. I suffer a little pruning to just keep me on track to my destiny." Every day she rises to the knowledge that God loves her; even in her current condition. She can reach out and touch a new world of people she had no desire to access months ago.

> She is the lady who has God's Word on her mind and His Word for every situation. She has become a street corner preacher. Her territory is any city on which she sets her feet. She has made a name for herself among the homeless for they trust her, and she believes she has been called by God and equipped with His Word to help change their "lost status" into homeless, but loved.

Ally does not offer promises of grandeur or miraculous recovery. She admits that the world is a tough place to navigate. She has amassed a shopping basket of resources. The first item she hands out is a Bible, the second is the Word of God. She speaks out to those who are counted among the lost with a gift of "the good news" of the gospel! She stands everyday on the restorative Word of God. The once soft-spoken educator now walks among her students. She teaches English to non-speakers and helps with resumes. She helps children with homework and makes sure they are first in line when the food lines start to form. She knows how to file for aid, housing, and clothing assistance. She knows the correct answers that will get a response from the social services offices. She knows who is working among the exiles and gives a Bible to those who make it back to social society.

By everyone's standard she is still "connected" to the corporate world. Someday she may choose to travel on the path that leads back to society's acceptable standards for the educated PHD. Of all this she says, "Like restoration, elevation comes from God and is not directional. Sometimes we have to step down to step up! It's simple," she says. "It's not about your walk; it's all about your worship!"

Go past your current worship to what God originally wanted for you. He will restore anything that was lost when you elevate your worship.

Ready to write?

Today's Date:

_____

_____

_____

_____

_____

_____

_____

_____

_____

_____

_____

_____

_____

_____

_____

_____

Day 12

Enhance Your Worship

Purpose:

To remind us that God's requirement for obedience is crucial for continual receipt of blessings and service to Him.

Hearing the Word:

1 Samuel 15:22-23

[22] But Samuel replied: "Does the LORD delight in burnt offerings and sacrifices as much as in obeying the LORD? To obey is better than sacrifice, and to heed is better than the fat of rams.
[23] For rebellion is like the sin of divination, and arrogance like the evil of idolatry. Because you have rejected the word of the LORD, he has rejected you as king."

Story:

We read in Isaiah 44:24, *"I am the Lord, Maker of all things."*
God is the ultimate authority over His creation. This
scripture, taken from 1 Samuel 15, is about the ultimate
disobedience. God has given Saul a direct order which he
does not carry out. In fact, he (Saul) does the opposite of
what was requested of him. God has asked him to destroy
something, which Saul has decided should be used instead
as a sacrifice. The question posed to Saul by Samuel is,
which is a better offering to the God who created all things
-- your obedience, or burnt offerings?

Obedience is better than sacrifice. We are instructed in
scripture to obey those in authority over us. The
disobedience of a nation reigns throughout Israel's history.
The reward for obedience is that you will enhance your
worship every time! God has given us proof that He would
rather we obey by offering His only begotten Son as the
last required sacrifice.

We have a choice to guard and to offer our obedience to
God. There are consequences outlined in the scripture for
not obeying God. The scripture states, *"Rebellion is like the
sin of divination and arrogance like the evil of idolatry."* We show
our parents that we understand their instructions or
directions by carrying them out to the fullness of our
ability. 1 John 5:2-3 states, *"By this we come to know (recognize
and understand) that we love the children of God: when we love God
and obey His commands (orders, charges) – when we keep His
ordinances and are mindful of His precepts and His teachings".*

Our love for God is shown when we keep His
commandments. Our rebellion is sin. Choosing to serve

and obey God is choosing against sin. We can choose not to idolize people or things, because there is a better sacrifice to be made. Paul in Romans 12:1 stated the following: "I appeal to you therefore, brethren, and beg of you in view of (all) the mercies of God, to make a decisive dedication of your bodies (presenting all your members and faculties) as a living sacrifice, holy (devoted, consecrated) and well pleasing to God, which is your reasonable (rational, intelligent) service and spiritual worship." God would rather that we give Him our hearts; mind, body and soul in our daily worship and choose to walk with Him than the material things of this world (which have no life) that He also has authority over. Created in His image, we are His representatives on this earth. This representation flows across all aspects of our lives.

The term "team player" has become essential to how the business world works. Team members are expected to answer to those in managerial authority. Team members are also selected based on their ability to support the project and team in a professional manner. Team meetings are set up to discuss project problems. Team leaders are the first line of communication when problems occur. Disobedience and organization chaos occurs when a team member takes his problems to higher management without following the hierarchical managerial flow set in place to handle such events.

Saul rejected the Word that God had given him and followed his own path. God was the authority to whom Saul had agreed to submit and to follow. God did not give Saul the authority to alter His instructions. Like Saul, we should choose God's Word over our own. Proverbs 3:5 says, *"Trust in the Lord with all your heart and lean not to your own understanding. In all your ways acknowledge Him, and He will make your paths straight."* The bible as our instruction outlines our path. God orders our way. God's Word is protection against evil, arrogance, and idolatry. Not following the line of authority places us in the path of sin.

King Saul disobeyed God and was rejected as the King of Israel. God had an expectation that Saul would honor Him and reign under His authority. In the business world, there is an expectation that we will follow the authority set in place. Saul offered excuses for his behavior for not following the instructions as God had outlined. Samuel cried out to the Lord for Saul's misdeeds, but later delivered the judgment to Saul that God had outlined.

It is true that we have choices. Sometimes our choice is as simple as being followers; even when we are the leaders or experts in our field.

Ready to write?

Enhance™ Inventory		
Encourage yourself	Handle your hang-ups	Center your thoughts
How can you encourage yourself to obey God?	List 1-3 ways that you can obey God more sincerely?	How may you think about that temptation in a more godly way?

70

Today's Date:

_____

_____

_____

_____

_____

_____

_____

_____

_____

_____

_____

_____

_____

_____

_____

_____

_____

_____

_____

_____

_____

Day 13

Acceleration of Your Worship

Purpose:

To discover what is required to move you from where you are to the place of true worship and the presence of God.

Hearing the Word:

Psalm 103:1; Psalm 95:1-2; Psalm 100:1-4

[1] Bless the LORD, O my soul; and all that is within me, bless His holy name!

[1] Oh come, let us sing to the LORD! Let us shout joyfully to the Rock of our salvation. [2] Let us come before His presence with thanksgiving; let us shout joyfully to Him with psalms.

[1] Make a joyful shout to the LORD, all you lands! [2] Serve the LORD with gladness; come before His presence with singing. [3] Know that the LORD, He is God; it is He who has made us, and not we ourselves; we are His people and

the sheep of His pasture. ⁴ Enter into His gates with thanksgiving, and into His courts with praise. Be thankful to Him, and bless His name.

Story:

When we read Psalm 103, we are reminded that God is the source of all our blessings. This scripture points out David's desire to bless God with his whole being. When we express our praise, it should be done with our whole being – body, soul and spirit. Our entire life should be a psalm of praise to God.

A Scottish poet named Horatius Bonar penned a hymn that says:

> Fill Thou my life, O Lord my God,
> In every part with praise,
> That my whole being may proclaim
> Thy being and Thy ways,
> Not for the lip of praise alone,
> Not even a praising heart
> I ask, but for a life made up
> Of praise in every part!

Our whole lives ought to be a psalm to God – our whole spirit, soul and body. Spirit is the part of us that brings us into the Holy of Holies and into the immediate presence of God; where real worship happens. The soul is made up of the mind, the emotion and the will. It should be affected by our spirits when they are in touch and in fellowship with God; it's where worship is expressed to God. The body is the place where praise is expressed, and when we praise God, it should be done with enthusiasm.

We can see the progression of praise in Psalm 95 as it begins with loud jubilant praise. This type of praise comes with a noise that may not be tolerated in some or our churches. Making a joyful noise really means to shout joyfully – not so much about loud singing, but loud shouting in the house of God! This type of praise is meant to be a celebration, to extol God in His greatness, and it's done in an exuberant, unrestrained manner.

Unfortunately, this type of praise can be misinterpreted and may also be misunderstood. Sometimes when someone really starts getting excited and praising God, folks may think they're exhibitionists or they're being self-centered and showoffs. While that may be true for some, this can never be an argument for *not* giving the praise and the true worship that is due to God. To be certain that this type of praise and worship is genuine and true, it's good to follow this principle:

God-consciousness will cast out self-consciousness.

In other words, the more conscious you are of God's presence, the blinder you will become to the presence of those who are around you; blind to embarrassment in front of them, and blind to impressing them, if you happen to be the type of person who may be prone to self-centeredness.

When David praised God, he danced until he became naked before the ark, he was not concerned with self-consciousness. When the sinner woman in Simon the Pharisee's house came before Jesus, broke the alabaster box

75

and anointed his feet with that precious ointment, and then washed his feet with her tears and dried his feet with her tears, she was not self-conscious or embarrassed. If either of them had been self-conscious, neither of them would have been able to freely do what we see recorded in the scriptures.

When that precious alabaster box was broken and the fragrance released, all the restrictions and restraints were released with it. In order for that which is the most precious to be freely released in you, the precious box has to be broken. There may be restraints and restrictions to exuberant praised and worship, and we may feel the spirit of worship welling up within our souls, but if something is confining that praise and worship, then that is what needs to be broken so that the perfume of the Spirit may rise and come forth and our worship be accelerated.

As your worship accelerates, you will discover that it also encourages the miraculous, it wins battles, and it drives the enemy away. It's praise that heals the soul and calms the troubled spirit. The most important thing that praise does is, when it's combined with thanksgiving, it gives us access to God. There are two degrees of access to the presence of God – first through His gates, and secondly into His courts, as it states in Psalm 100:4. If you would ever desire to accelerate you worship to move into God's presence, you first have to enter through the gates and then move into the courts; His gates with thanksgiving and His courts with praise.

An excellent example of accelerated worship is the story of George Frideric Handel, and the way in which he came to compose the awesomely timeless song, *The Messiah*, of which the Hallelujah chorus is the most famous and most frequently sung. Handel was born in Germany in 1685. As he grew up, he had a tremendous desire to compose operas. This desire compelled him to relocate to Italy where opera was prevalent. Unfortunately, the pope, at that time, banned opera, believing that secular and sacred music should not be tolerated. Still desiring to compose music for operas, Handel eventually moved from Italy to Britain where he became a naturalized citizen in 1727 and a famous composer of sacred music.

By the age of 52, Handel had suffered a debilitating stroke, which incapacitated him by paralyzing his right arm (he was right-handed) and blurred his vision. Also, Handel was not a very wise businessman and had lost a large fortune in the opera business. Being depressed and in debt, Handel decided that he should give up. He was at his lowest point. Shortly after all these calamities, he discovered a libretto (opera lyrics) that had been written by Charles Jennens, which was divided into three compelling parts:

1. Prophecies about the coming Messiah;
2. The birth, life, ministry, death, and resurrection of Christ; and
3. The end times with Christ's final victory over sin and death, as it is written in the book of Revelation.

He was so inspired by what he read, he decided to try once more to write the oratorio (music with voices) based on this libretto. He all but barricaded himself into his room and practically neither ate nor slept the entire time as he wrote *"The Messiah"*. When he got to the Hallelujah chorus, his assistant found him in tears. Handel said, "I believe I saw heaven open, and saw the very face of God. It seemed as if heaven came down and filled my soul."

Handel's *The Messiah* soon became very popular and was quickly established as a classic piece. I'm sure he never would have anticipated that this work would become perhaps the most performed piece of classical music in all of history; all to the glory of Christ. He certainly could not have anticipated the many variations and versions of the performance of *The Messiah*.

This is the power of praise and true worship and a testament of acceleration in worship. Consider what should be broken in your life so that the spirit of praise and true worship can be released.

Ready to write?

Today's Date:

_____

_____

_____

_____

_____

_____

_____

_____

Day 14

Worship Builds My Relationship with God and I Will Produce Fruit
(Blessing, anointing, prophecy, deliverance and healing, kingdom authority, strategies, ambassadorship)

Purpose:

To understand that true worship cannot be restrained by what others think, and it will ultimately result in God's favor upon our lives.

Hearing the Word:

Psalm 103

[1] Praise the LORD, my soul; all my inmost being, praise his holy name. [2] Praise the LORD, my soul, and forget not all his benefits—[3] who forgives all your sins and heals all your diseases, [4] who redeems your life from the pit and crowns you with love and compassion, [5] who satisfies your desires with good things so that your youth is renewed like the eagle's. [6] The LORD works righteousness and justice for all

the oppressed. [7] He made known his ways to Moses, his deeds to the people of Israel: [8] The LORD is compassionate and gracious, slow to anger, abounding in love. [9] He will not always accuse, nor will he harbor his anger forever; [10] he does not treat us as our sins deserve or repay us according to our iniquities. [11] For as high as the heavens are above the earth, so great is his love for those who fear him; [12] as far as the east is from the west, so far has he removed our transgressions from us. [13] As a father has compassion on his children, so the LORD has compassion on those who fear him; [14] for he knows how we are formed, he remembers that we are dust. [15] The life of mortals is like grass, they flourish like a flower of the field; [16] the wind blows over it and it is gone, and its place remembers it no more. [17] But from everlasting to everlasting the LORD's love is with those who fear him, and his righteousness with their children's children—[18] with those who keep his covenant and remember to obey his precepts. [19] The LORD has established his throne in heaven, and his kingdom rules over all. [20] Praise the LORD, you his angels, you mighty ones who do his bidding, who obey his word. [21] Praise the LORD, all his heavenly hosts, you his servants who do his will. [22] Praise the LORD, all his works everywhere in his dominion. Praise the LORD, my soul.

Story:

Here is the greatest invitation I can give to you, the greatest gift I can offer you: one that has no expiration date, time or place. Come worship and praise the Lord with me! An invitation is extended from me to you. If for some reason you choose not to worship the Lord with me, understand this: I will worship Him all by myself!!

The psalmist in this scripture displays the excitement of one who has been the recipient of God's unlimited love! I can identify with his excitement. No repentant person, having been born again, knowing the salvation of our Lord God, can reject the invitation! If you have a relationship with God, you too have a testimony to the love and greatness of God! God's unmerited favor (grace) is wonderful, and He has shared it with the church (His body), with the world (through His spoken Word), and with His children (His creation)!!

We speak of our worship and our worship services being "off the chain!" I suppose another way to put it is, the word of our testimony is so powerful that we enjoy sharing it with other believers. Our God has shown His greatness, His majesty and His power in our lives directing our feet along the path of right-mindedness for His glory and His purpose. We want to share it with the world community.

Allow me to bring to your remembrance the message of the benefits of worshiping God. This psalm outlines them well. It speaks of forgiveness and restoration of health. It reminds us of our Redeemer and the mercies of God. Spiritual joy resides in this psalm. Spiritual joy is a subset of everlasting joy! In this Psalm David discusses with himself the good and goodness of God, over which his soul should rejoice.

Think of those down times when you (and your relationship with God) had to talk yourself through a troubling situation. Remind yourself about how God brought you through some things like no human man could. You had to "encourage" yourself!

Spiritual Joy allows you to encourage yourself, knowing that:

- Joy is gladness and is not based on circumstances
- With joy, sorrow and suffering will flee
- Joy breaks forth with singing, shouting, dancing and praising
- Joy is an emotion that cannot be commanded by others
- Joy is an action that can be engaged in regardless of how a person feels
- Spiritual joy is without reference to circumstances or situations

Look within yourself and rejoice to the greatness of God. Praise God from within your soul because He is holy. Thank God for who He is; for He alone is God and greatly to be praised. For the Creator is able to:

- Forgive your sins,
- Heal you,
- Redeem you,
- Give you good things,
- Renew your strength,
- Justify you
- Have compassion on you, as a father has compassion on His children,
- Keep His covenants

It is His righteousness and sovereign rule that sustains you. He does this all from His throne in heaven, which He has said is also your home. He has breathed life into you and has given you dominion in His Kingdom. David sang praises to God, and worshipped Him in an unprecedented way which we find admirable. David praised so intently that he danced out of his clothing. The relationship David had with the Lord was intently on his mind, heart and soul. David worshiped God from the inside out; not the outside in. He did not care what he looked like, nor did he care what others thought of his praise.

This Psalm is about the attitude David had toward God. God is greater than all His creation, including the angels and man. Vertical worship (true worship) does not include a horizontal look at the world. Only God is being worshiped.

John 4:23-24 speaks to all true worshippers:
"A time will come, however, indeed it is already here, when true (genuine) worshippers will worship the Father in spirit and in truth (reality); for the Father is seeking just such people as these as His worshippers!!"

God is seeking us as His worshippers!! God is a Spirit (a spiritual Being), and those who worship Him must worship Him in spirit and in truth (reality). This is what we see in how David worshipped God.

On the day of Pentecost, over 3000 were saved. On that day many were recipients of the Holy Spirit's flaming presence. They spoke in tongues, as the Spirit enabled them.

David worships God in spirit. God is a spirit and must be worshipped in spirit and truth. How many services have you attended where the Holy Spirit was so strong on a person that the person danced uncontrollably, or could not stand under His loving power, or takes off running around the room. The heaviness of the Spirit requires that person to surrender to the power of God. It is the vertical relationship with God that enables the person to enter into such powerful worship. The Holy Spirit wraps Himself around these people and indwells their praise, which is strictly between them and God.

Ready to write?

Today's Date:

_____

_____

_____

_____

_____

_____

_____

_____

_____

_____

_____

_____

Day 15

Singing As Worship

Purpose:

To know that songs of praise and worship release us from those things holding us captive.

Hearing the Word:

Psalm 100

> [1] Shout for joy to the LORD, all the earth.
> [2] Worship the LORD with gladness; come before him with joyful songs.
> [3] Know that the LORD is God. It is he who made us, and we are his; we are his people, the sheep of his pasture.
> [4] Enter his gates with thanksgiving and his courts with praise; give thanks to him and praise his name.
> [5] For the LORD is good and his love endures forever; his faithfulness continues through all generations.

Story:

For those among us who cannot sing, the bible instructs us to make a joyful noise to the Lord in Psalms 98! Here in Psalm 100 we are told to shout for joy to the Lord with gladness. All the singing and shouting is about the goodness that God lavishes on those to whom He has shown His love, mercy and unmerited favor. All the earth should worship the Lord. We should see God in all that He has created. We should never be without something to say about the greatness of God. We should not come into the presence of God silent or empty-handed. We bring our songs and our joy to lay before Him. How can we not rejoice when the Words of God are in our mouth, and in speaking forth we acknowledge that He is God? When we do not have the joy of the Lord or cannot acknowledge the things around us which He has created for our joy and the wonders of His handiwork, we are held captive in our thoughts, our troubles, our trials, and the world that was void and dark which He transformed with the Words, "Let there be." To use our "get out of this dark, dank jail" that we have created, we must turn and worship God in His holiness.

I am sure that the jail Paul and Silas were held in was nothing like the one we create when we fail to see the love of God for us. A jail story is forth coming. It is a jail experience unlike any other but suffices to show the love and goodness of God. A friend starts the story off this way: I remember the one time I agreed to go to jail. [Remember she said, "I agreed" to go to jail.] It was for a good cause that I made such a thoughtless, selfless decision. It was a sorority function that (at the time of conception) seemed a good thing to do. The local police

86

department had agreed to participate in helping us raise money for a children's home. The rules were very simple:

1. We would be picked up from campus (a visual showing of our incarceration);
2. Taken to jail (where we would sit in a jail cell for photographic ops);
3. The local radio station would announce that we were in jail and could not be released until someone volunteered to donate X-dollars to the home, and therefore, secure our release.
4. Once the money had been secured at the radio station (that had agreed to match the funds we raised), it would announce that we were free and had done this noble thing to help others.

The off-duty arresting officer was married to one of the sorority members. This was a great combination, for publicity, and raising funds--sorority girls sitting in jail with real criminals, waiting on the community to bail them out. Paul and Silas sang songs, just as we did. They were also physically bound. That is the extent of the similarities between the two events. We knew that we would be free to walk out at any time.

Take a closer view of the faith at work that both Paul and Silas had in God. What they went through has helped generations of believers. They were physically bound (their feet were fastened to the stocks), but they were not spiritually bound. They made a joyful noise to God through singing hymns and prayer, and at midnight they prayed. This impacted others who were listening to them. Everyone was set free. Their chains were lessened allowing them freedom. The wonderful thing that happened was that the jailer was saved unto God that night.

Luke 15:10 says, *"I tell you that in the same way there will be more rejoicing in heaven over one sinner who repents than over ninety-nine righteous person who do not need to repent."*

My friend said of her experience: "I do know that a shout for joy went up when I was released!" I believe that for Paul and Silas' experience there would have been rejoicing in heaven.

We should enter the church every Sunday with thanksgiving and praise. Our worship should intensify because the Lord brings us together to a place of worship. The sanctuary should be loud with our outward praise and alive with our worship. Chains should fall away because of our prayer and relationship with Him. We should confess the greatness of God in our lives and present ourselves as sacrifices holy unto Him. We should humbly honor Him as our Creator. This worship should be renewed daily as we should seek our place as Kingdom citizens worshipping our Father collectively.

Ready to write?

Today's Date:

_____

_____

_____

_____

_____

Day 16

My Worship Will Turn Me Into Another Person

Purpose:

To understand that true worship is able to transform and give you a new direction.

Hearing the Word:

Philippians 3:13-14; 1 Samuel 10:6

[13] Brothers and sisters, I do not consider myself yet to have taken hold of it. But one thing I do: Forgetting what is behind and straining toward what is ahead,
[14] I press on toward the goal to win the prize for which God has called me heavenward in Christ Jesus.

[6] The Spirit of the LORD will come powerfully upon you, and you will prophesy with them; and you will be changed into a different person.

Story:

In order to get to worship, we have to move beyond the ideals of the world, pressing toward worship beyond praise and enter into a realm that is only reserved for God and you. Your presence before God does not have a "look" to it. You don't have to maintain a level of dignity. David danced so uncontrollably (giving no thought to what he looked like) that he danced out of his clothes. True worshippers know what it is like to stand before the presence of God. True worshipers know what it is to stand in God's presence. Praise can lead you there (as in the outer court), but worship allows you to enter in (the Most Holy Place). There are songs that help one in praise, but the precursor to worship is words that witness to God's great deeds and His glory.

As we press forward to become who God has pruned and shaped us to be, the level of our worship changes. We are no longer on milk. The thirst is quenched at that level and we have to know and follow God's plan for growth displayed in our acknowledgement of Christ and the work God is doing to transform our lives.

My worship is integral to my transformation. The higher my praise and worship, the greater joy I have when I press toward God's plan. I become a new, repentant person with salvation and deliverance as my companions. I walk humbly acknowledging God's gifts and will for my life, over which He has dominion. I accept responsibility for the kingdom territory which He has allotted to me, based on my faith in Him. Every day is a day in which honor should be bestowed upon God.

> We become a Leader not a follower
> We become an effective prayer warrior
> We become an intercessor
> We study God's Word
> We proclaim God's Word
> We share the love of God with others
> We build the body of Christ
> We build the church

Seeking God and His kingdom requires attention from God and action on our part. We come into His presence through worship. It is here where:

- Our worship allows God to raise a standard on our behalf for us to connect to.
- As you press toward the mark of the high call, the results you achieve will be fulfilled through your decisions.
- Your vision will determine what areas to exercise discipline (an internal decision and personally executed standard with a desire to attain a higher goal). Your success will be the result of how your decisions and discipline connect to your goals.
- You connect to God and others by:
    - The way you love
    - Your character (ways)
    - Your worship and praise
    - Your words
    - Your witness

- God wants to connect us to His vision, passion and goals…so **PRESS** toward that mark of your high calling in Christ Jesus!!

The Bible is alive with people who were transformed when God extended himself to their call. Paul is a great example, because he turned completely away from a life in which he excelled to a life doing the work of God among people who were not God's chosen people. Paul, through the inspired Word of God, given to him, continues to affect the lives of millions today.

People who stood in the presence of God have had their lives changed forever. This is the transformation we seek.

Ready to write?

PRESS (Version 1) ™ Inventory		
Prepare	Express	Sustain your worship
How may you press toward the mark through your worship?	List 1-3 ways that you may sincerely express gratitude toward God?	How may you sustain your worship all day long today?

Today's Date:

_____

_____

_____

_____

_____

_____

_____

_____

_____

_____

_____

_____

_____

_____

_____

_____

_____

_____

_____

_____

_____

_____

_____

_____

Day 17

Miracles, Signs and Wonders Will Follow a Worshipper

Purpose:

To understand that our praise and worship should never cease because only God knows our final outcome.

Hearing the Word:

Acts 5:12-16

[12] The apostles performed many signs and wonders among the people. And all the believers used to meet together in Solomon's Colonnade.
[13] No one else dared join them, even though they were highly regarded by the people.
[14] Nevertheless, more and more men and women believed in the Lord and were added to their number.
[15] As a result, people brought the sick into the streets and laid them on beds and mats so that at least Peter's shadow might fall on some of them as he passed by.

97

¹⁶ Crowds gathered also from the towns around Jerusalem, bringing their sick and those tormented by impure spirits, and all of them were healed.

Story:

Greater is He that is in me than he that is in the world. Truly I believe that almighty God created the heavens, the earth, and all mankind. I believe that God is still creating, He is alive and well, and He is living in and through His people.

The apostles performed wonders among the people. Today many are looking for the big miracle. Ask people to describe a miracle, and they will say it requires seeing the impossible happen right before their eyes. However, miracles take place every day. Birth is still a miracle in which God bears witness to Himself. We were created in His image, and through birth the creation cycle continues. We have gotten so accustomed to this miracle, that it has become commonplace. Instead, we wait for the *big* miracle; the one that man cannot produce and that only God can. Jesus walking upon the waters was indeed a miracle that has not been reproduced by man. Peter was the only man who partook in this miracle; but only temporarily, because his faith failed him.

For us, Christ's resurrection and defeat of death, which gives the believers a victory of eternal life, is the greatest miracle. In the book of Revelation, John speaks of the signs that indicate the return of the Messiah to battle with Satan. Wondrous things are described during this battle in which we can take confidence that we are victors and have already won. Read the book of Revelation and receive the blessing of having done so.

Paul speaks of the relationship with Christ which allowed him to minister to the world and do those things that Christ had done during His walk among the people. Worship takes us into the presence of God. Jesus states in John, chapter 10:9 that, *"I am the door; by me if any man enter in, he shall be saved, and shall go in and out, and find pasture."* The story of Paul and Silas is one about how worship brings us into the presence of God, we get God's attention, and He shows us His power. In this narrative their chains fell away, and the guard repented and found new life and salvation unto Christ.

Disciples and ambassadors bring God's lost children home through living and proclaiming His Word. This is a miracle whose end result (the repentant sinful soul returned to God) is worth heavenly celebration. One benefit of our praise is its elevation into worship.

The miracles of our day may go unnoticed, for they have become everyday events in our lives. Someone walking on water would become the norm over time and go without notice, just as the miracle of flight beyond our planet has become. The miracle of birth is no longer held in high esteem. We still seek greater, more impressive miracles from God. The signs of Jesus' return are always at the forefront of the unknown as man tries to delineate through the environment around him. Several have even predicted this, but all fall short of the knowledge of God. Look closer for the miracles, signs and wonders of God. You may very well find that the workings of God in your life are a miracle. Daniel experienced a miracle when God delivered him from the lion's den. Consider the healing miracles you have witnessed in your life time.

There have been many times when people have lived beyond what was pronounced over their life. Doctors had told Will that he had only 3 months to live because the tumor he had was not responding to the prescribed treatment. Will then prepared a place for his eternal rest, told his family and friends what was going on within his physical body, and then said goodbye to his best friends. He had "made peace" with the Lord.

He cautiously noted that his three months became six months; and then the 6 months became one year. Three years later, Will still proceeded thorough his daily life with the thought that it would end any day. One day he realized that everyone lived as he did; from day to day. Will decided that worry would not help his situation. So, he resolved to believe that only God knew the exact day on which He would call Will homeward. This to us is the miracle that we can identify with. Like Will, we must choose to acknowledge that only God knows His plan for our lives.

Worship God with thanksgiving in the beauty of His holiness.

Ready to write?

PRESS (Remix)™ Inventory			
Personal Worship	Reaching up to Christ	Experience Miracles	Signs and Wonders follow
Define your bold personal worship?	How will you look to Jesus to teach you today?	How will you look for the moves of God around you?	List 3 signs and wonders of God!

Today's Date:

_____

_____

_____

_____

_____

_____

_____

_____

_____

_____

Day 18

God is the Source of Everything – I Worship Him

Purpose:

To provide assurance that the Creator understand the needs of His creation and sees and makes provision accordingly.

Hearing the Word:

Philippians 4:19-20

[19] And my God will meet all your needs according to the riches of his glory in Christ Jesus.
[20] To our God and Father be glory for ever and ever. Amen.

Story:

God is our Father, forever. The beginning of this scripture includes the possessive pronoun, "my." This speaks of the relationship between the Creator and His creation. The normal relationship is to have the Owner speak of His creation in reverse. The creation speaks of its submission to the Creator. This brings us into relationship with God. God supports and approves my relationship with Him, so I will worship Him in His righteousness. James says that you have not because you do not ask.

God is our source for every need. Prayer is the means through which we commune with God. Praise allows us to thank God for what He has done for us, and when we enter the realm of worship, it acknowledges God as Ruler over our lives. We belong to Him and seek to be worthy of this honor. The bible states, *"Let the redeemed of the Lord say so."* So, we say this through praise songs and dances. We say so through prayer and through worship. We enter into God's presence acknowledging Him for His unmerited grace, for we are created in His image. We are not creators; we are created, still dependent upon His mercy and grace for sustainment and survival. God is our Source, our Provider, our Protector, and He is love. The very breath in our bodies belongs to and is regulated by God. He alone knows our beginning and our end.

Everyone loves babies; they are tiny, helpless, newly born life forms. They are the created of God. From the time of Cain and Abel, we have all entered the world the same way. God is the source of our being, and only God can create and sustain life. It still amazes us that the baby in the womb takes a first breath after it is born into the world. It grows into a full being then is delivered into the world. God is waiting upon that delivery to give the breath of life to this infant. Without God's breathe, there is no life.

God interacted in creation with the universe. The trees in the garden were assigned to carry life and sustain fruit. Two particular trees are mentioned in the biblical account of creation: the Tree of Life and the Tree of the Knowledge of Good and Evil. Both trees are secure in Eden, but man (the God seed) has been expelled from the garden. This seed (the seed of Adam) had required forgiveness, redemption, deliverance and salvation provided by God. Sin has taken away from the loving joy of being eternally in God's presence. The physical status in Adam and Eve held before their encounter with the serpent in the garden was greatly altered when God removed them from the garden.

Just as its fruit knew the tree in the garden, so a child of God is known to be fruitful by the exhibition of our indwelling faith. So, Adam and Eve (and all mankind) began to multiply as the tress through the seed. God said to them, to Abraham, and to us, *"Be fruitful* (have the character of God) *and multiply."*

God is the source of our "fruitfulness and our multiplication." Being fruitful, we display and adorn the character of God. God is a Spirit; therefore, the spirit within us should have the character of God. The fruit of the Spirit defines our character. The Apostle Paul in his letter to the Galatians said, *"But the fruit of the Spirit is love, joy, peace, forbearance, kindness, goodness, faithfulness, gentleness, and self-control."* To this we add the knowledge of God's character. God is Spirit. God is the invisible Spirit, in Hebrews described the evidence of things not seen.

John 1:18 states that, *"no one has ever seen God, but the one and only Son, who is Himself God and is in closest relationship with the*

Father, has made him known." So, it is only through Jesus that we have a clearer understanding of who God is. Through scripture God has admonished that we should lean not to our own understanding, but acknowledge Him in all things. We acknowledge that we were created in His image. Our character can be seen before our physical bodies enter a room.

Quiet often I have entered a room or a conversation that is altered simply by my presence; or shall I say, simply by the presence of God in me. The conversation changes to being more peaceful. The yelling and name-calling ceases; all because the "image" and characteristic fruit of God has entered the room. We are to alter situations by entering into them.

The same can be seen when Jacob wrestled before the Jabbok River. I understand the theologian and Bible scholarly view of the events that took place at that time for Jacob. It could have been possible that Jacob was wrestling with his own character. He had not treated Esau fairly, and now he had to come to terms with what he had done. The wrestling was with an angel whom God had sent to reconcile Jacob unto himself. At the end of this encounter both Jacob and Esau received a blessing. Esau went along his way to settle in another land also. Jacob knew that God was the Source of all his possessions.

We say we work hard for the things we have, because you have them and God has worked hard to give them to you. Sharing the wealth that God has lavished on you is a wonderful attribute for sharing and acknowledging your relationship with God. Worship acknowledges the understanding you and all of your possessions are the possession of God.

Pray, giving thanks and supplication to God!

Ready to write?

Today's Date:

_____

_____

_____

_____

_____

_____

_____

_____

_____

_____

_____

_____

_____

_____

Day 19

Worship Brings Me Into God's Presence

Purpose:

To know that true worship brings you into God's presence and urges you to want to see others in that place also.

Hearing the Word:

Psalm 132:7; Revelation 4:1-11

⁷ Let us go to his dwelling place, let us worship at his footstool, saying, …

> ¹ After this I looked, and there before me was a door standing open in heaven. And the voice I had first heard speaking to me like a trumpet said, "Come up here, and I will show you what must take place after this."
> ² At once I was in the Spirit, and there before me was a throne in heaven with someone sitting on it.
> ³ And the one who sat there had the appearance of jasper and ruby. A rainbow that shone like an emerald encircled the throne.

4 Surrounding the throne were twenty-four other thrones, and seated on them were twenty-four elders. They were dressed in white and had crowns of gold on their heads.
5 From the throne came flashes of lightning, rumblings and peals of thunder. In front of the throne, seven lamps were blazing. These are the seven spirits of God.
6 Also in front of the throne there was what looked like a sea of glass, clear as crystal. In the center, around the throne, were four living creatures, and they were covered with eyes, in front and in back.
7 The first living creature was like a lion, the second was like an ox, the third had a face like a man, the fourth was like a flying eagle.
8 Each of the four living creatures had six wings and was covered with eyes all around, even under its wings. Day and night they never stop saying: "'Holy, holy, holy is the Lord God Almighty,' who was, and is, and is to come." 9 Whenever the living creatures give glory, honor and thanks to him who sits on the throne and who lives for ever and ever,
10 the twenty-four elders fall down before him who sits on the throne and worship him who lives for ever and ever. They lay their crowns before the throne and say:
11 "You are worthy, our Lord and God, to receive glory and honor and power, for you created all things, and by your will they were created and have their being."

Story:

God is omnipresence. Worship is personal when entering into His presence. Our limitless God is present everywhere! We do not come into God's presence; we are always in God's presence. David asked the question best in his Psalm 139:7, *"Where can I go from your Spirit? Or where could I flee from your presence?"*

110

In today's transient world, families are spread out in cities across a nation. One brother might live in Alabama, while a sister may reside in New York. The truth is, these two siblings are still related to one another; no matter their location. Although they can't always see each other, the connection is still there and that connection is still a vital part of their family history.

God knows each one individually. God, being omnipresent, can see what is going on in the daily lives of each child. Though separated from each other, they are both always in God's presence. God continues to interact with both, where they are, and to the degree of their faith, and obedience. God knows what our earthly home looks like and uses scripture, dreams and visions to impart to us the knowledge of what heaven looks like. Worship is about God and who He is; not about mankind and who we are. God is worthy of all honor and glory because He created; not because of what He created.

We are His handiwork. David acknowledges that God knows everything about His creation and has total control and authority over all things. It is David's worship that brought him into God's presence. David wrote psalms that were powerful and humbling, and were specifically about his spiritual relationship with God.

God explained to Job that He has created and continued to control everything around him. This act of giving life and creating life is worthy of worship and recognition beyond just praise. Often God will supply our needs as an answer to our prayers. We request that God supply a way out of our troubled situations. This request is made after we have attempted to make a way to handle the situation ourselves. A loving and forgiving God takes over and handles our lives as His children are seeking His consolation. The reward is passed down to us, as thankful worship and supplication flows upward to God.

Great organizations have been birthed to help those in need. There are often more people in need than the organization's ability to help them. In times of dire crisis, people, through love or belief, will step up to take on a cause. Often these organizations exist within the church. God supplies their needs so that they can pass those blessings on to others.

Joanna is a spirited woman of God. She sings in the choir, along with her husband Jimmy and three sons. She dances for the Lord on most church 4th Sundays. She truly knows the blessing of a "helping hand" in today's economically depressed society. She and her husband Jimmy were recipients of organizational blessings as children. The organizations supplied clothing when their parents could not. The organizations supplied food to help out when their parents could not. The need was greater doing the holiday season than any other time of year.

The couple was grateful and prayed that God would allow them to be helpers to His people in some way. She would say, "God opened a door for us in our time of need. He will use us to help others. He will allow our story to be the fuel to help other families temporarily unable to make it day to day by society's standards." Jim would say, "God blessed our family in times of our need. We knew that in some way He would allow us to help others. So, we prayed for His direction, and He heard us."

As their children grew up, funding became easier to acquire to help others in need. Together they prayed that God would show them how to help others through troubled times and situations. Joanna and Jim were directed to help as many people as they could by feeding and clothing them. She would prepare Sunday dinner and take it to a local area where she knew families gathered to shelter themselves from the pains of life and hardships of the world.

They prayed that God would allow them to provide for other families and "after Sunday worship meals" that would change their lives. They sought out areas where families had set up temporary shelters. Bridges offered more shelter from the environment, so they would look there. It was not long before they found makeshift shelters beneath a bridge. They would deliver the hot meals; sit down with the families; pray for God's blessing, goodness and grace; and then eat. She said, "Although I wanted to, I would not invite them to church because they would be shunned by church goers and thought of as different, lazy, dirty and not wanted." Yes, and some of them did fit all of those descriptions; but in Joanna's eyes, they were still children of God.

So, for the first year, she and Jim spent Sunday evening preparing meals for and eating with the homeless families they called the Bridge family. The numbers of families (adults with their children) who would appear under the bridge grew over time. Families would come and wait on the two of them every Sunday. They had been careful to get the word out that, they were interested in helping families. The meals included prayer and study time. Several families did join her church.

As God supplied the funding to her family, Joanna and Jim supplied the meals and the Word of God to the people. The meals she prepared were identical to the ones she prepared for her family. They were hot, balanced, and plentiful. She and Jim had raised boys, and she knew that once through the serving line would not be enough for them. So, God supplied funding to buy enough that most could make two trips through the food line.

Over time, she began to invite her church family to have dinner with her bridge family. They were surprised at the address she gave them, at the quality of the food she served, and even more at the number of families who showed up for dinner. Eventually, other church families wanted to help out because, they too, had been through dire circumstances that only God had been able to bring them through. God had the key to the heart that brought them together.

On Sunday evenings everyone knows where to find Joanna. God called Jim home. The families that live under the bridge have changed over the years. A few returned to society, but with organizational help they were able to get help. Joanna delivers the meals alone to the families that live under the bridge. She has had to cut back, both financially and physically, on the number of days she cooks for them; but the quality of the meals remains the same.

The stories around the table revolve around God. God is the supplier of our needs, and when we don't ask amiss, He provides. Heavenly God sits on His throne and knows the needs of His children. God enables us to provide for others sharing what we have received. Prayer, supplication and thanksgiving bring us into God's presence.

Don't stand before God empty handed. Graciously bow in spirit and allow Him to use you. Give glory and honor where glory and honor are due, as worship to the Lord. Speak of the greatness of God in your life by offering your worship and proof that He is worthy. Follow and believe in the scripture, for it is alive and lives within you! Speak of the love and giving graces of God. Join with the heavenly elders and shout to the Lord:

> [11] "You are worthy, our Lord and God,
> to receive glory and honor and power,
> for you created all things,
> and by your will they were created
> and have their being

Worship the Lord our God, for He will supply your every need!

Ready to write?

Today's Date:

_____

_____

_____

_____

_____

Day 20

Worship As Adoration

Purpose:

To understand that worship transcends denomination and we can all love God the same; in spite of how we appear to be different.

Hearing the Word:

John 4:21-26

[21] "Woman," Jesus replied, "believe me, a time is coming when you will worship the Father neither on this mountain nor in Jerusalem.
[22] You Samaritans worship what you do not know; we worship what we do know, for salvation is from the Jews.
[23] Yet a time is coming and has now come when the true worshipers will worship the Father in the Spirit and in truth, for they are the kind of worshipers the Father seeks.
[24] God is spirit, and his worshipers must worship in the Spirit and in truth."

[25] The woman said, "I know that Messiah" (called Christ) "is coming. When he comes, he will explain everything to us."
[26] Then Jesus declared, "I, the one speaking to you—I am he."

Story:

The Father seeks worshipers! Jesus in His conversation with this woman, wanted her to know that, who she was (Jew or Samaritan), did not matter, because a time is coming when all people will worship one God. Those who blindly worship God (who do not know Him, but follow the practices of man), will soon worship as the Jews do with the knowledge that God is Father to all people. Worshipers will come to God as little children, as His children.

Robin recounted to me the times as a child when she was allowed to visit her best friend's church. The church was of a different denomination. Her parents were concerned about the difference, but she could not understand their questions, since her friend didn't seem to be that different. She had heard adults introduce themselves as a "this" or a "that," meaning they were attached to a specific denomination and church roll. The truth was, Robin did not really care about her friend's "denomination." She simply liked her and thought she was someone cool to be around.

The church services were a little different, heavily laden with tradition, history and pomp. Robin found one thing most interesting, beyond the quiet and slumbering praise music; she noticed that they used the same bible as her church. It started in Genesis and went through to Revelation. The ministers talked about the same disciples, the same Abraham and Adam, and the same Paul that she had learned about at her church! Worshiping God was the primary focus of the service. She never thought much after that about their services. Her worship of God did not change because of her environment. Her relationship with God was vertical and horizontal.

Samaritan believers are still among our ranks. They know and dote on the traditions and rituals of the church. They are of the mindset that all they need to do is check the "I go to church" box; tell everyone, "Yes, I entered the building and said amen six times, waved at the Pastor and got all the latest gossip on sister so-n-so;" and everything is good. They have not repented their sins and been born again unto God. They would agree with the Samaritan woman that Christ is coming to explain it all to them-someday.

True worshipers MUST worship in spirit and in truth. We would pray that someday they may discover that worship is serving in spirit and submitting your hearts, thoughts and actions over to God. God is so worthy of adoration and truthful worship! We should bow before His throne daily and seek to emulate Jesus in His humility. We will face trials and troubles, but they do not interfere with our worship of God.

We worship and adore God for being God. Worship can be a celebration to God. Jesus prayed, and scripture often states that He found places of solitude to spend time in prayer to God. God is love, and this should be displayed in our worship. Jesus responded to the Samaritan woman regarding her statement of waiting on the Messiah to come to explain everything to us. The good news is that the Messiah has come, and the explanation is clear and true – adore and joyfully worship God!

Ready to write?

Adorre™ Inventory		
Adoration	**Observation**	**Reach higher expectation**
List three reasons to adore God?	How have you observed others worship in the scriptures?	What will you do to reach a higher expectation of adoration toward God?

Today's Date:

_____
_____
_____
_____
_____
_____

Day 21

Worship Gives Me Security and Victory

Purpose:

To know that God stands outside of our human limitations, and worshipping Him assures victory, in every circumstance.

Hearing the Word:

Exodus 4:31; 12:24-27; Ephesians 3:14-21

[31] and they believed. And when they heard that the LORD was concerned about them and had seen their misery, they bowed down and worshiped.

[24] "Obey these instructions as a lasting ordinance for you and your descendants. [25] When you enter the land that the LORD will give you as he promised, observe this ceremony. [26] And when your children ask you, 'What does this ceremony mean to you?' [27]then tell them, 'It is the Passover sacrifice to the LORD, who passed over the houses of the Israelites in Egypt and spared our homes

when he struck down the Egyptians.'" Then the people bowed down and worshiped.

[14] For this reason I kneel before the Father, [15] from whom every family in heaven and on earth derives its name. [16] I pray that out of his glorious riches he may strengthen you with power through his Spirit in your inner being, [17] so that Christ may dwell in your hearts through faith. And I pray that you, being rooted and established in love, [18] may have power, together with all the Lord's holy people, to grasp how wide and long and high and deep is the love of Christ, [19] and to know this love that surpasses knowledge—that you may be filled to the measure of all the fullness of God. [20] Now to him who is able to do immeasurably more than all we ask or imagine, according to his power that is at work within us, [21] to him be glory in the church and in Christ Jesus throughout all generations, for ever and ever! Amen.

Story:

The scripture begins *"and they believed."* The Israelites believed that Moses was sent by God to do a good work. They believed that God knew their condition and had responded to them by sending Moses with a message for them.

Bowing before God gives Him the honor for our success. It is submission to a greater, loving power. Bowing, kneeling or lying prostrate is a humble, state of physical submission to a superior, a master, or Lord. The people in this scripture first believed in the messenger sent before God on their behalf. They knew God had responded to their request, and they knew the correct and proper response for God. Today we bow down and worship with prayer and thanksgiving, knowing and believing that He hears and responds to our every need.

I am reminded of the story of my friend who needed gas for her car to get to work. She had neither gas nor the money to get it. She stopped in at a local gas station and then parked her car at the pump, knowing that she had no funds with which to buy fuel. Before going into the market, she said a prayer to God. "God", she said, "you know my circumstances. Lord you know that I need to get to this place, but I have no money. God I am counting on you to help me through this." God said to her, "Look under your foot." When she moved her foot there was a $10 bill lying on the ground next to her foot!

Another story that comes to mind is one about the power of submission and prayer to God. This is about a friend who needed groceries for her son. She and her sister were not speaking to each other, so she had no family to call. She kneeled down to pray to God about her situation. While praying, the doorbell rang and she reluctantly got up to answer. The person at the door was a friend from church. She said, "Sorry to bother you, but I need your help. I know that you are a praying lady, and I just need prayer for my daughter. She has gotten herself in trouble and when I thought about asking someone to pray for her, your name came to mind." The friend said, "Yes, I will pray for her." As the lady walked away, my friend closed the door to resume her prayers. The lady came back and knocked at the door again. This time she said, "Well, you know how I like to shop when I am under pressure. I went by the store and bought more food than I can use. Can I get you to take the food?"

Worshiping God in the stories and scripture is bowing down to Him. Bowing acknowledges that a greater God had provided a way for success. It is acknowledging that the God of all creation is greater than His creation! We honor God with reverential fear, and therefore, reverential honor. This is our way of showing love, obedience and submission. The name on which we boast is the Name of God; not man.

The outlined scriptures bring to mind the scripture that asks God to explain, *"Who is man that You are mindful of him."* God is so immense that it is hard for our brains to understand the enormity of His being. Our understanding is based on our self-limitations. We can be in only one place at a time, but God is everywhere. We cannot limit God by our own human standards. We are totally dependent upon God for life. Miracles, signs and wonders are His products. God has redeemed mankind from salvation to salvation; yet we keep coming back for more.

God hates sin, and man has previously sold himself into sinful ways. Having been "tricked" once by Satan, and then bought for a price, man has the sinful ungodly nature to which he succumbs. Satan has been convicted and cast out by God. Man still awaits his destiny. He has the victory, but it is often said of Satan that he will take as many human souls with him as possible.

We should shout from the rooftops that we have the victory! Eternal life is ours! Yet mankind often chooses to go against the Word of God and gives up his eternal home. How man understands his relationship with God is evident in the choices he makes. There will be problems and conflicts, but at the end of the day, God remains sovereign.

Worship is a deeper, spiritual connection to God. It honors the indwelling spirit and allows for a true spirit-to-spirit connection. It is the only way to worship God. John 4:24, instructs us that God is a spirit and his worshipers must worship in the Spirit and in truth. The truth that Paul prayed and that the Ephesians would gain, through prayer and obedience, was that:

1. God would strengthen them internally with power through His Spirit,
2. Christ might dwell in their hearts through faith; and
3. Being rooted and established in love, they might have the power to know God's love that surpasses knowledge—that they might be filled to the measure of all the fullness of God.

Are these not the same desires we have today, for those engaging in a vertical relationship with God? It is our knowledge of who God through instruction, obedience and submission, as worshippers, we also acknowledge that only God is worthy. God is omnipotent, Omniscient, and Omnipresent, and He is worthy of our worship.

God responds to us through our worship. In our times of trouble, He will provide a way for us – not because He has to, but because He is able. God alone is able to keep us from falling. He provides our salvation through repentance. We are washed clean in the blood of His Son, Jesus Christ, who has presented us faultless in His glorious presence. All things were made by God, and nothing that He has made can separate us from His love.

127

It is this love that Paul notes with this knowledge establishes us in His love and allows us to excel in living a more holy life,

Shout to the heavens that, in our repentant state, we have been given a victory that manifested itself on the cross. We have the victory over death provided through Jesus' life, resurrection and death on the cross. Our victories come daily. We must continuously seek God and His Kingdom. We must die to self in order to be alive in Christ.

I am secure in the Word of God, which is established in all truth. I am an heir of God through Jesus Christ. Whatever I bind on earth is bound in heaven, and whatever I loose on earth is loosed in heaven. As children of the Most High God, we have the authority and power to carry forth Jesus' work.

Ready to write?

Vict'or'ee™ Inventory		
Victory	**Overcomer**	**Equip to Excel**
List three victories you have had recently?	How did you overcome?	How has God equip you to excel in living a more holy life?

Today's Date:

_____

_____

_____

_____

_____

_____

_____

_____

_____

_____

_____

_____

_____

_____

_____

_____

_____

_____

_____

_____

Conclusion

Like love, prayer is an imperative – we are commanded to pray, just as we are commanded to love. Becoming a person of prayer is to fulfill your obligation to reaching and sustaining a true relationship with God. It was the expectation that this book, *21 Days of Life*, would be the catalyst to assist you in effecting that change.

When we know God's plan through prayer, but we fail to practice it, then we are just like the person that is spoken of in James 1:22-25; we can see our reflection when looking into a mirror, but as soon as we turn away from that mirror, we forget what we look like. We were created in the image and likeness of God. We should; therefore, be a reflection of what He looks like and who He is. The only way to fully know what that looks like is to be in a committed relationship with Him and faithfully follow His Word through prayer and practice. Turning away from God and not desiring to be in His presence through prayer, is just like turning away from a mirror; it puts us in a place where we forget what we look like.

My challenge to you is that you will take this book and consistently begin praying according to the Word of God and in the Name of Jesus. Discover your power and authority, and discover that as you grow in prayer, your rights as an intercessor will also begin to grow. You *will* become a powerful individual of prayer.

Worship can make a significant difference in one's life. Worship makes known how much God is worth to us. It is our love connection to our Maker and Creator. Worship brings certainty to our relationship with God and His people.

When we worship, we let God know that we adore Him, recognize we are in the hour of true worship and recognize that God is looking for such a people to worship. Becoming a worshipper will cause a change in your life and be a blessing to your future. Also, the Word of God birthed out of an intimate relationship with God is worship.

We may come to know God more deeply and strongly through our worship. However, when we worship in the spirit, we will come to know and recognize His thoughts, will and way for our lives.

I trust you have enjoyed your journey with this book. As stated in the Introduction, the intent of this book is to demonstrate how we live and how we are made better because of a true relationship with Jesus Christ our Savior.

Again, when you have true worship, there is intimacy with God, Himself. This relationship will birth:

- Blessing
- Anointing
- Shalom (Peace)
- Prophecy
- Deliverance and healing
- Miracles, signs and wonders
- Kingdom authority

Thank you for taking this daily journey. I trust your life is transformed and that you have a deeper walk with God through Jesus, after this daily interaction.

It is guaranteed that, through a daily commitment to prayer, your life will be changed, your relationship with God will be enhanced, and you will see the difference that this will make in your worship. Now that you have reached the end of the 21 days, you will read it again and again. Also, please share with your kingdom sisters and brothers how God has done marvelous things through this time with Him.

End Notes

Day 1:

1. Webster Online Dictionary: Domain. <u>www.merriam-</u>
<u>webster.com/dictionary/domain</u>.

About the Author

Dr. Amanda H. Goodson is a native of Decatur, Alabama and currently resides in Tucson, Arizona where she is a leader in her church. She has been employed for major contractors in Arizona for over 10 years. As a Senior Executive for the National Aeronautics and Space Administration (NASA), she was Director of the Safety and Mission Assurance Office at the Marshall Space Flight Center (MSFC) in Huntsville, Alabama.

God has gifted Dr. Goodson to be a Spirit-led preacher, teacher, trainer and coach for churches, and faith based groups. She gives God glory as He allows her to inspire others to learn more about being a Spirit led Kingdom Ambassador in the world today. She is the host of the Bountiful Life television program, which is designed to reach female audiences in the Tucson, Arizona, community between the ages of 20 to 70 years, in order to take them from where they are to where they are purposed to be. She is a published author of several books.

Dr. Goodson has a Bachelor of Science degree in Electrical Engineering, a Master of Science degree in Management, and a Doctor of Ministry.

She and her family enjoy their ministry work for the Kingdom.

For further information or to book **Dr. Goodson,** please contact her at:

AmandaGoodson.com

Books by Dr. Amanda Goodson

Spiritual Quickbooks [TM]
Kingdom Character
Spiritual Authority
Carmel Voices
The Power to Make an Impact
Powerful People Follow Christ
Step out in Faith
Going Higher, Declarations for Kids
On the Rise
Spiritual Intelligence
Switch to Holiness

Spiritual Workbooks
Switch to Holiness Workbook

Leadership Minibooks [TM]
The Authority of a Leader
Character of a Leader
Unlock Your Full Potential
12 Power Principles for Administrative Professionals
Soar to Your Destiny

Leadership Workbooks
Unlock Your Full Potential Workbook

135

www.ingramcontent.com/pod-product-compliance
Lightning Source LLC
Chambersburg PA
CBHW072024040426
42447CB00009B/1725